Walter Einstein

Airbnb Business Blueprint: The Ultimate Guide to Starting and Succeeding in the Airbnb Business.

To All My Readers
I dedicate this book to all aspiring entrepreneurs and Airbnb enthusiasts who are ready to embark on their journey of starting an Airbnb business. This book intends to furnish you with the information, direction, and motivation expected to succeed.

"A place is not home; it's a sensation of having a place, and Airbnb has reclassified that inclination for millions all over the planet."

Contents

Preface 1

1. Acquiring Knowledge of the Airbnb Business Model.............................3

2. How to Start an Airbnb Business 7

3. Finding the Right House 9

4. Enhancing Your Listing 11

5. Conveying Uncommon Visitor Encounters.............................15

6. Efficiency in Operations Management 18

7. Showcasing and Advancing Your Airbnb Business.................22

8. Scaling Your Airbnb Business 26

9. Guaranteeing Legitimate Consistence and Hazard The executives 28

10. Exploring Difficulties and Making Long haul Progress.......................29

11. Conclusion 34

1.

2.

3.

4.

5.

6.

7.

8.

9.

10.

11.

Preface

The world of Airbnb entrepreneurship is yours to explore!

The ascent of the sharing economy has changed the manner in which we travel, associate, and experience new spots. Airbnb has emerged as a powerful platform in the midst of this transformative wave. It allows people like you to become hosts and create one-of-a-kind lodgings that meet travellers' varied requirements and preferences worldwide.

This book is a comprehensive guide that aims to show you how to start and grow your own Airbnb business successfully. This book will provide you with the knowledge, strategies, and practical insights necessary to thrive in the Airbnb marketplace's competitive landscape, whether you are an experienced hospitality professional looking to expand your reach or an aspiring entrepreneur making your first steps in the industry.

We will examine various aspects of the Airbnb business throughout these pages, including setting up your business, finding the ideal property, and optimizing your listings for maximum visibility, as well as comprehending the fundamental principles and advantages of the Airbnb model. We will investigate the art of providing exceptional guest experiences, effectively managing operations and putting marketing and promotion strategies into action.

This book also covers important topics like growing your business and overcoming legal and compliance obstacles. We will talk about how to manage multiple listings, expand your property portfolio, and comply with the law all while reducing risks and ensuring guest safety and security.

It's vital to note that this book isn't an assurance of a mind-blowing phenomenon. In order to build a successful Airbnb business, one must be dedicated, eager to learn, and willing to change with the times. You will, however, have a solid foundation from which to launch your venture and overcome any challenges that may occur along the way armed with the information and insights presented in these pages.

Remember that creating authentic, memorable experiences for your guests is the core of the Airbnb business as you embark on this exciting journey. It is through your enthusiasm, meticulousness, and obligation to give special friendship that you will separate yourself and construct a devoted client base.

I encourage you to read this book with an open mind, to take notes, and to apply the lessons and techniques to your own particular business vision. May it be useful as a helpful resource and direction as you work toward success in the Airbnb industry.

I wish you success and happiness in your Airbnb endeavours!

1

Acquiring Knowledge of the Airbnb Business Model

The peer-to-peer marketplace that connects travellers with hosts who are willing to rent out their homes or apartments is the foundation of the Airbnb business model. The company makes money by charging a commission on each reservation, which typically ranges from 5% to 15%, depending on how long the stay is and where the property is located.

What is Airbnb?

Airbnb is an online marketplace that connects travellers looking for a place to stay with people who want to rent out their homes, apartments, or rooms. By offering an alternative to traditional hotels and lodging options, Airbnb, which was established in 2008, has revolutionized the hospitality sector.

Hosts can list their homes and set their own rental conditions, such as availability, pricing, and house rules, through Airbnb. The traveller's desired location, travel dates, and specific preferences can search for accommodations. The platform lets guests talk to hosts directly, make reservations, and write reviews after their stay.

Airbnb offers an extensive variety of convenience choices, taking special care of different spending plans and inclinations. The platform offers a wide range of listings in cities and locations all over the world, including private bedrooms, shared rooms, and entire homes.

Airbnb's offerings now include experiences and activities hosted by locals in addition to lodging. Tourists can book unique experiences, such as cultural workshops, cooking classes, and guided tours to enrich their travels and connect them with the local culture.

Airbnb has had a significant impact on the travel industry by giving people the chance to monetize their properties and making it possible for travellers to have more individualized and immersive lodging experiences. It has gained popularity due to its ease of use, affordability, and capacity to connect hosts and guests from all over the world.

Importance of Starting an Airbnb Business

There are many advantages to beginning an Airbnb business. First of all, it can be a great way to make more money. It also lets you meet new people and let travellers from all over the world stay in your home. You likewise have the adaptability to set your own timetable and pick when you need to lease your space. The most important advantages include:

Extra Pay: Leasing your property or extra space on Airbnb permits you to create an extra stream of pay. This can be especially useful if you have extra space or a property that isn't being used.

Control and adaptability: You can choose when and how frequently you want to rent out your space as an Airbnb host. You can set your own accessibility, valuing, and house rules, giving you full command over your business activities.

Low Initial Costs: The initial costs of starting an Airbnb business are typically lower than those of starting a traditional lodging business. You don't have to put resources into gaining or fabricating a committed property since you can use existing space.

Contact a Worldwide Crowd: You can reach potential guests from all over the world through Airbnb's user-friendly platform. Your chances of consistently getting a reservation are increased by this global exposure, which can draw in a wider range of tourists.

Organizing and Social Trade: Facilitating visitors from various foundations can give open doors to social trade and systems administration. It lets you meet new people, learn about other cultures, and possibly make connections that matter.

Boosted Property Worth: Your home's value could rise if you keep your Airbnb listing popular and well-reviewed. Positive visitor audits and high inhabitance rates can make your property more interesting to purchasers or financial backers later on.

Use of the Property for Oneself: You can still enjoy your property for personal use when it is not rented out if you run an Airbnb business. You can earn money while enjoying the advantages of having a second or vacation home thanks to this flexibility.

Proficient and Innovative Turn of Events: Maintaining an Airbnb business requires unique abilities, like correspondence, friendliness, the board, showcasing, and critical thinking. Participating in these activities may help you develop your entrepreneurial and professional skills.

Possibility for Design and Creativity: It can be fun and creative to design and decorate your Airbnb space. You are free to create a one-of-a-kind and appealing setting that will draw in guests and set your property apart from others.

Community Assistance: Airbnb places a lot of emphasis on helping hosts develop a sense of community. Taking part in neighbourhood meetups, sharing experiences, and supporting each other can give a feeling of having a place and backing in your pioneering venture.

Because of these advantages, starting an Airbnb business is an appealing option for people who want to monetize their properties, make additional money, and participate in a flexible and rewarding entrepreneurial endeavour.

Challenges and Considerations of Starting an Airbnb Business

Although starting an Airbnb business can be a fantastic opportunity, there are certain obstacles and things to keep in mind. Because there are likely a lot of other Airbnb hosts in your area, competition is one of the biggest obstacles. As a result, you'll need to find ways to differentiate yourself and offer something unique. Cleaning, upkeep, and insurance are just a few of the expenses you'll need to think about when setting up and maintaining your Airbnb property. It's likewise vital to know about any nearby guidelines or regulations that might affect your capacity to work an Airbnb business. At long last, you'll should be ready to deal with any issues that might emerge with visitors, like abrogations or objections. In general, starting an Airbnb business can be rewarding, but before you start, it's important to carefully consider all of the obstacles and   factors.

2

How to Start an Airbnb Business

By obviously distinguishing what you need to accomplish with your business, you can make a guide for progress. This part will direct you through the most common way of putting forth sensible and quantifiable objectives that line up with your own yearnings and monetary targets. You will investigate a variety of factors to take into consideration, including the desired level of income, occupancy rates at the property, and guest satisfaction metrics.

Compliance with Various Legal and Regulatory Requirements

When operating an Airbnb business, it is necessary to abide by a variety of legal and regulatory requirements. You will learn how to navigate the necessary permits, licenses, and registrations and gain an understanding of the legal landscape surrounding short-term rentals in this section. We will investigate drafting guidelines, mortgage holder affiliation rules, and nearby regulations intended for your locale. You can operate your business with confidence and avoid potential legal issues by ensuring compliance.

Making a Strategy

A very much created strategy is fundamental for any fruitful endeavor. You will learn how to create a comprehensive Airbnb business plan in this chapter that includes information about your strategies, target market, competition analysis, marketing strategy, and financial projections. You will find the resources and direction you need in this section to create a solid plan that will guide your business's growth and success. You will figure out how to direct statistical surveying, recognize your special selling recommendations, and set sensible achievements.

Funding Your Airbnb Business

Funding is a critical part of beginning and scaling an Airbnb business. This part will dive into different subsidizing choices accessible to you, from individual reserve funds and advances to elective supporting strategies. You will figure out how to evaluate your monetary requirements, foster a spending plan, and investigate expected wellsprings of financing, including customary banks, financial backers, crowdfunding stages, and taxpayer supported initiatives. Understanding the monetary part of your business will empower you to pursue informed choices and secure the important assets to fuel your development.

Establishing a Professional Team

It often takes a dedicated team of professionals to run a successful Airbnb business. In this section, you will learn how to build a team that is competent and trustworthy and can help you manage various operations. We will talk about key jobs like property supervisor, housekeeping staff, upkeep work force, and visitor support agents. You will learn about how to hire people well, how to train people, and how to build a team culture that works together. In addition, the options for outsourcing and utilizing third-party services to boost your business's efficiency will be discussed   in   this   section.

3

Finding the Right House

Identifying Ideal Locations

T he best place to live for an Airbnb is in the right place. You'll need to consider factors like vicinity to well-known traveller objections, public transportation, and neighbourhood conveniences like eateries and shops. You will be able to make well-informed decisions that are in line with your business objectives and target market if you have a thorough understanding of the distinctive features and requirements of various neighbourhoods.

Property Types: Apartments, Houses, and More

Understanding the various property types that are available for your Airbnb business is essential after you have identified potential locations. We will dive into the advantages and disadvantages of condos, houses, apartment suites, and other property choices. You'll learn about the particular things to think about for each type, like size, amenities, maintenance needs, and who they are for. With this knowledge, you can choose the best type of property based on your budget, target market, and long-term objectives.

Evaluating Property Listings

Effectively evaluating property listings is essential if you want to locate the ideal property. There are a few important things to think about when looking at Airbnb property listings. You should look at the property's location and amenities first and foremost. You should also think about the property's size and whether it can comfortably accommodate the number of guests you want to host. Last but not least, you should check the property's price and availability to make sure it meets your company's requirements.

Arranging Lease Arrangements

An essential step in securing your Airbnb property is negotiating lease agreements. This section will furnish you with fundamental discussion methodologies and bits of knowledge to assist you with exploring lease arrangements effectively. We'll talk about important things to include in the agreement, like the length of the lease, the amount of the rent, security deposits, and who is responsible for the maintenance. By understanding the discussion cycle and being ready, you'll have the option to get good rent terms that line up with your business goals.

Assessing the Property's Needs for Renovation and Furnishing

Following the conclusion of the lease agreement, you will need to evaluate the property's requirements for renovation and furnishing. In this section, you'll learn how to assess the property's condition, figure out what needs to be done, and make a budget for the costs of improvements. We'll look at ways to make the most of available space, improve aesthetics, and make your guests feel at home. In addition, we'll talk about cost-effective options for furnishing and how to find high-quality furniture and decor within your budget.

4

Enhancing Your Listing

Creating a Compelling Posting Title and Portrayal

In order to attract potential guests to your Airbnb business, it is essential to create an irresistible listing title and description. Your title should be catchy and descriptive, highlighting your property's distinctive qualities. Your property's amenities, location, and any unique features that set it apart should all be detailed in your description. Using high-quality pictures to show off your space and make it more appealing to potential guests is also important. The most important listing title and description are;

1. Recognizing the significance of a catchy listing title
2. Choosing keywords that are engaging and descriptive
3. Highlighting distinctive features and services
4. Using powerful language to make an emotional appeal
5. Keeping the title short and to the point
6. Making an appealing description that highlights the property's advantages, features, and location
7. Writing in a way that convinces and captivates
8. Using language that is focused on the guest and addressing their wants and needs
9. Making use of subheadings and bullet points for ease of reading
10. Incorporating nearby landmarks and tourist attractions
11. Displaying favourable guest ratings and reviews
12. Optimizing your listing's title and description through A/B testing and refinement

Taking Pictures of High Quality

High-Quality Photography High-quality photographs are worth a thousand words when it comes to attracting guests. In this section, we'll talk about how to take captivating photos that show off your property's best features and make a strong first impression.

1. Preparing your property for a photo shoot
2. Choosing the right lighting and equipment
3. Framing and composition for maximum impact
4. Showcasing each room and highlighting unique details
5. Using natural light to create a warm and inviting atmosphere
6. Including lifestyle shots to give guests a sense of experience
7. Editing and enhancing photos to ensure visual consistency
8. Uploading photos to your Airbnb listing and strategically arranging them
9. Regularly updating photos to reflect any improvements or changes.

Setting Prices That Compete

It is essential to set a reasonable price for your Airbnb listing in order to both attract guests and ensure profitability. In this section, we will discuss efficient methods for establishing pricing that is competitive, reflects your property's value, and maximizes occupancy rates.

1. Performing market research to comprehend local pricing trends
2. Comparing comparable listings in your area
3. Taking into account seasonal fluctuations and demand patterns
4. Identifying peak periods and adjusting prices accordingly
5. Offering competitive rates while taking overhead costs into account

6. Using Airbnb's pricing tools and algorithms
7. Strategically offering discounts and promotions
8. Monitoring and adjusting prices based on performance and guest feedback
9. Using pricing optimization tools and software for data-driven decision making
10. Executing dynamic estimating techniques

Making Use of the Programs for Airbnb Plus and Superhost

The programs for Airbnb Plus and Superhost give your listing more benefits and credibility, which helps you get more guests and get higher occupancy rates. In this part, we will investigate how to use these projects to improve your posting's permeability and notoriety.

1. Understanding the qualification standards for Airbnb In addition to Superhost status
2. Preparing your property to meet the necessities
3. Showcasing your property's exceptional highlights and conveniences
4. Conducting an intensive self-evaluation to satisfy Airbnb In addition to guidelines
5. Complying with the Superhost models for outstanding visitor encounters
6. Leveraging the identifications and upgraded permeability that accompanies these projects
7. Promoting your Airbnb In addition to Superhost status in your posting and advertising materials
8. Utilizing the extra advantages and assets accessible to In addition to and Superhost individuals

Enhancing Listing Visibility and SEO

It is essential to optimize your Airbnb listing for search engine optimization (SEO) and increase its visibility on the platform for maximum exposure and booking potential. In this part, we will investigate compelling systems to help your posting's permeability and draw in additional visitors.

1. Figuring out the significance of Website optimization in Airbnb rankings
2. Directing catchphrase research and consolidating applicable watchwords in your posting
3. Advancing your posting title, portrayal, and conveniences for Website optimization
4. Using Airbnb's pursuit channels and elements for your potential benefit
5. Empowering visitor surveys and utilizing them to further develop rankings
6. Answering instantly and expertly visitor requests and messages
7. Using Airbnb's limited time includes and supported postings
8. Executing off-stage promoting systems to direct people to your posting
9. Observing and dissecting posting execution measurements
10. Keeping awake to-date with Airbnb's calculation changes and stage refreshes

By carrying out the strategies illustrated in this section, you will actually want to streamline your Airbnb leaning to draw in additional visitors, stand apart from the opposition, and increment your booking rates and income.

5

Conveying Uncommon Visitor Encounters

Making an Inviting Climate

Making an inviting climate is fundamental for any fruitful Airbnb business. To accomplish this, you'll need to zero in on the little subtleties that have a major effect, for example, giving open bedding, new towels, and smart contacts like nearby suggestions or a welcome crate. It's likewise vital to keep the space spotless and very much kept up with, and to discuss plainly with visitors to guarantee their visit is charming.

Significance of a warm and welcoming space: A warm and welcoming space is fundamental for making an inviting environment in your Airbnb. It can assist visitors with feeling good and at ease during their visit.

Planning an inviting inside: Planning an inviting inside can include picking the right tones, furniture, and stylistic layout to make a comfortable and welcoming space for visitors.

Using individual contacts and scrupulousness: Individual contacts and meticulousness can have a major effect on making a vital visitor experience. This can incorporate things like giving new blossoms, customized welcome notes, and insightful conveniences.

Upgrading control allure and initial feelings: Improving check allure and initial feelings can assist with drawing in expected visitors and establishing a good first connection. This can include things like finishing, outside lighting, and a very much kept-up outside.

Making a significant visitor appearance experience: Making a noteworthy visitor appearance experience can include integrating every one of the above components to make a warm and welcoming space that visitors will recall long after their visit.

Recognizing the Expectations of Guests

A key part of running a successful Airbnb business is knowing what to expect from guests. Guests want a place to live that is neat, comfortable and has everything they need. This includes amenities like clean sheets, towels, and toiletries, as well as entry to a kitchen that is fully furnished and dependable Wi-Fi. Additionally, guests often appreciate when hosts provide thoughtful welcome gifts and local recommendations.. In addition, it is essential to respond to guest inquiries and concerns and to provide clear and comprehensive check-in and check-out instructions. You can build a solid reputation and attract repeat business by putting guest satisfaction first and exceeding their expectations.

Providing Essential Amenities

Guests anticipate and ways to go above and beyond to meet or exceed their requirements. From giving essential necessities like towels, toiletries, and a completely prepared kitchen to offering extra conveniences like diversion choices, clothing offices, and outside spaces, we'll direct you in making an excellent visitor experience.

Communication and Guest Assistance

Effective communication and guest assistance are essential for a pleasant stay. Best practices for communicating clearly and promptly, providing assistance and recommendations, and professionally handling guest requests and feedback will be discussed in this chapter. By proactively tending to visitor needs, you can have an enduring positive impression and develop major areas of strength for a.

Taking care of Visitor Audits and Criticism

Visitor surveys and criticism assume a huge part in moulding your Airbnb business' standing. We'll talk about how to handle both positive and negative guest reviews and how to use feedback to improve your property and service. Also, we will investigate strategies for empowering visitors to pass on audits and utilizing positive surveys to draw in additional appointments.

You can build a reputation for providing exceptional experiences by understanding and exceeding guest expectations. This will result in positive reviews, more bookings, and greater success for your Airbnb business.

6

Efficiency in Operations Management

Streamlining Reservation and Booking Systems

For any Airbnb business to be successful, it is essential to simplify the booking and reservation systems. To accomplish this, bookings, payments, and guest communication must be managed using effective software and tools. To ensure the safety and satisfaction of guests, it is also essential to uphold high hygiene and cleanliness standards. This incorporates standard cleaning and sanitizing of the property, giving clean cloths and towels, and guaranteeing legitimate ventilation. Overseeing registration and look at processes is one more significant part of maintaining an Airbnb business. This entails giving guests clear instructions, making certain that the check-in procedure runs smoothly and effectively, and collecting necessary data like identification and payment information.

Keeping Standards of Cleanliness and Hygiene

Keeping up with tidiness and cleanliness norms is a basic element in beginning and maintaining a fruitful Airbnb business. It's essential to lay out clear rules and assumptions for visitors, as well as execute ordinary cleaning and sanitizing conventions to guarantee a protected and agreeable stay for everybody. This covers:

1 Making a cleaning agenda: Foster a far-reaching agenda to guarantee all regions of your property are cleaned completely.

2 Setting high tidiness principles: Lay out rules for your cleaning staff or for yourself on the off chance that you handle cleaning obligations.

3 Teaming up with cleaning administrations: Investigate choices for recruiting proficient cleaning administrations to reliably keep up with neatness.

4 Occasional upkeep and investigations: Carry out schedules to recognize and address any support issues instantly.

Overseeing Check-In and Check-Out Processes

Managing check-in and check-out processes is a critical factor in running a successful Airbnb business. It's important to have clear communication with guests about arrival and departure times, as well as provide a smooth and efficient check-in and check-out experience. This can help ensure a positive guest experience and lead to positive reviews and repeat bookings. This gives experiences into:

1 Fostering a smooth registration process: Plan a consistent registration experience for your visitors, remembering key trade or self-check-for techniques.

2 Giving clear guidelines: Impart directions and subtleties to visitors before their appearance to keep away from any disarray or deferrals.

3 Upgrading look-at methodology: Smooth out the look-at process by giving reasonable aid on how visitors ought to leave the property and return any keys or access cards.

4 Gathering criticism and audits: Urge visitors to give criticism on their registration and look at encounters to work on future activities.

Executing Viable Safety Efforts

Executing viable safety efforts is essential to guarantee the security and inner serenity of your visitors. This incorporates

1 Surveying property security: Assess your property's weaknesses and go to suitable lengths to upgrade security, like introducing surveillance cameras, vigorous locks, and caution frameworks.

2 Visitor confirmation: Carry out visitor check cycles to guarantee the well-being of your property and forestall fake exercises.

3 Security gear and methodology: Get to know neighbourhood wellbeing guidelines and furnish your property with smoke alarms, fire dousers, and crisis contact data.

4 Information security and security: Shield visitor data and conform to information insurance guidelines.

Managing Visitor Issues and Compromise

As an Airbnb have, you might experience different visitor issues and clashes. This segment gives techniques to successfully dealing with these circumstances, including:

1 Dynamic correspondence: Keep up with open lines of correspondence with your visitors and speedily address any worries they might have.

2 Critical thinking outlook: Take on a critical thinking way to deal with finding commonly good answers for visitor issues.

3 Intercession and compromise: Learn strategies for intervening in struggles between visitors or settling questions among visitors and neighbours.

4 Overseeing troublesome visitors: Foster methodologies to deal with testing visitor circumstances with amazing skill and beauty.

5 Visitor fulfilment and audit the executives: Focus on visitor fulfilment and influence positive surveys to improve your standing.

By productively dealing with your tasks, you can give outstanding encounters to your visitors and increment the outcome of your Airbnb business.

7

Showcasing and Advancing Your Airbnb Business

Building a Web-based Presence

In this section, we will investigate the significance of laying out major areas of strength for a present for your Airbnb business. We'll examine the different stages and systems that can assist you with contacting a more extensive crowd and drawing in expected visitors.

1. Figuring out the meaning of online permeability
2. Make a convincing Airbnb profile
3. Advancing your posting for web indexes
4. Exhibiting your property with top-notch photographs and portrayals
5. Using proficient photography and virtual visits
6. Creating a connection with and useful property site
7. Saddling the force of website streamlining (Search engine optimization)
8. Using Internet booking stages and property aggregators

Utilizing Web-based Entertainment Promoting

Web-based entertainment has turned into a fundamental piece of our lives, and it presents a gigantic chance for showcasing your Airbnb business. In this part, we'll dive into the systems and best practices for utilizing virtual entertainment stages to advance your postings and draw in possible visitors.

1 Distinguishing the most reasonable web-based entertainment stages for your ideal

    interest group

    2 Make a powerful online entertainment showcasing system

    3 Creating connecting with content and utilizing narrating

    4 Structure a steadfast local area of supporters and backers

    5 Using force to be reckoned with advertising to enhance your span

    6 Drawing in with clients through remarks, messages, and audits

    7 Running web-based entertainment challenges and advancements

    8 Checking web-based entertainment investigation and upgrading your endeavours

Publicizing and Advancements

To build the permeability of your Airbnb business, you might have to put resources into designated publicizing and limited-time crusades. In this part, we'll investigate different promoting channels and systems that can assist you with contacting your ideal crowd and boosting your appointments.

1 Figuring out various promoting choices, including on the web and disconnected

    channels

    2 Make viable promotions that feature the one-of-a-kind elements of your property

    3 Focusing on unambiguous socioeconomics and interests through crowd division

    4 Using pay-per-click (PPC) publicizing efforts

5 Working together with nearby the travel industry sheets and objective promoting
associations

6 Taking part in movement exhibitions, expos, and occasions

7 Checking publicizing execution and changing systems in like manner

Cooperating with Neighborhood Organizations and Powerhouses

Building organizations with neighbourhood organizations and powerhouses can essentially help your Airbnb business' permeability and validity. In this segment, we'll investigate how to distinguish and team up with important accomplices to extend your scope and draw in additional visitors.

1 Recognizing possible neighbourhood organizations and powerhouses in your space

2 Drawing nearer and laying out commonly helpful associations

3 Cross-advancing with corresponding organizations and administrations

4 Facilitating nearby occasions and encounters

5 Contribution exceptional limits and bundles through associations

6 Utilizing force to be reckoned with showcasing efforts to contact new crowds

7 Observing the progress of associations and sustaining continuous connections

Amplifying Positive Verbal exchange

One of the most remarkable promoting apparatuses for any Airbnb business is positive verbal. In this part, we'll talk about systems to make remarkable visitor encounters that urge visitors to impart their positive encounters to other people.

1 Zeroing in on remarkable client assistance and customized encounters
    2 Empowering visitors to leave audits and tributes
    3 Answering quickly and expertly visitor input
    4 Executing reference and reliability projects to boost proposals
    5 Displaying visitor tributes and audits on your internet-based stages
    6 Drawing in with nearby networks and encouraging positive connections
    7 Utilizing visitor criticism to work on your contributions and administration quality

By executing the systems illustrated in this section, you'll have the option to really showcase and advance your Airbnb business, increment its permeability, and draw in additional visitors, prompting a higher inhabitance rate and at last, better progress in the momentary rental industry.

8

Scaling Your Airbnb Business

Totally! Scaling your Airbnb business is a significant stage in developing your property portfolio and expanding your revenue sources. It includes recognizing open doors for extension, fostering a strong strategy, and carrying out powerful promoting procedures to draw in additional visitors. Also, it might include recruiting extra staff and putting resources into innovation to smooth out activities and further develop visitor encounters.

1. Extending your property portfolio is a savvy method for becoming your Airbnb business. This includes tracking down new properties to list on the stage and overseeing them really.

2. Dealing with different postings and activities can be testing, however it's fundamental for scaling your business. This incorporates monitoring reservations, cleaning timetables, and visitor correspondence across various properties.

3. Recruiting and preparing staff is significant for giving magnificent visitor encounters and keeping up with high tidiness and cleanliness principles. This incorporates employing cleaners, property directors, and client support agents.

4. Investigating co-host and property the executives administrations can assist you with smoothing out your activities and save time for different errands. These administrations can deal with everything from visitor correspondence to cleaning and support.

5. Enhancing revenue streams is a brilliant method for expanding your income and lessen risk. This can incorporate contribution extra administrations like air terminal pickups or visits, or in any event, putting resources into different kinds of land.

9

Guaranteeing Legitimate Consistence and Hazard The executives

Generally! Guaranteeing legitimate consistence and chance administration is urgent while maintaining an Airbnb business. It's vital to grasp neighbourhood regulations and guidelines, get fundamental allows and licenses, and have legitimate protection inclusion. Also, carrying out security measures and leading exhaustive visitor screenings can assist with relieving expected chances.

1. Charge commitments and guidelines are essential to comprehend to keep away from any legitimate issues or punishments.

2. Protection and obligation contemplations are critical to safeguarding yourself and your property from any possible harm or mishaps.

3. Taking care of visitor well-being and security is fundamental to guarantee a positive encounter for your visitors and to keep away from any expected lawful issues.

4. Managing lawful debates and compromise is vital to deal with any issues that might emerge with visitors or different gatherings engaged with your business.

5. Remaining refreshed on industry guidelines and changes is essential to guarantee that you are dependably consistence with any new regulations or guidelines that might influence your business.

10

Exploring Difficulties and Making Long haul Progress

Adjusting to Market Patterns and Contest

The Airbnb business is dynamic and continually developing. In this part, you will figure out how to adjust to showcase patterns and actually rival different hosts.

Figuring out market elements: Remain informed about industry patterns, changes in explorer inclinations, and developing business sectors. Ceaselessly screen the opposition and distinguish fruitful systems they utilize.

Developing your contributions: Routinely survey and update your property's conveniences, stylistic layout, and generally speaking visitor experience. Remain adaptable and open to visitor input, integrating ideas for development.

Estimating procedure: Keep your valuing serious by routinely assessing market rates and changing in like manner. Consider factors like interest, irregularity, neighborhood occasions, and your property's one of a kind selling focuses.

Showcasing and marking: Foster areas of strength for a personality that separates you from the opposition. Utilize convincing narrating and visuals to exhibit your property's novel elements and feature the encounters visitors can anticipate.

Dealing with Irregularity and Market Changes

Irregularity and market vacillations can essentially influence your Airbnb business. This is the way to explore these difficulties and keep up with reliable achievement:

Grasping occasional interest: Dissect verifiable information and examples to recognize high and low seasons in your space. Change your valuing, least stays, and promoting systems in like manner to draw in visitors during slow periods.

Broadening your objective market: Investigate different explorer sections to limit the effect of occasional variances. For instance, target business explorers, occasion participants, or families during off-top periods.

Offering advancements and bundles: Make alluring arrangements and bundles to captivate visitors during low-request periods. Team up with neighborhood attractions or organizations to offer packaged encounters and limits.

Anticipating appeal periods: During top seasons, advance your evaluating and accessibility to augment income. Execute least stays and change rates to reflect appeal.

Improving and Remaining Ahead

To prevail over the long haul, it's urgent to remain on the ball and consistently improve. This is the way to cultivate development and keep an upper hand:

Innovation reception: Embrace arising advancements to smooth out tasks and upgrade the visitor experience. Execute savvy home elements, mechanized registrations, and computerized specialized devices.

Upgrading visitor encounters: Persistently look for ways of further developing the visitor experience. Present customized proposals, one-of-a-kind conveniences, and unique contacts that put your property aside.

Manageability drives: Integrate eco-accommodating practices into your activities, like energy-proficient apparatuses, reusing programs, and mindful waste administration. Take care of the developing interest in reasonable travel encounters.

Remain refreshed on industry patterns: Go to industry meetings, join online networks, and understand industry-figured pioneers to remain informed about the most recent patterns, best practices, and innovative progressions.

Fostering a Practical Plan of Action

Building a reasonable plan of action is vital to long-haul achievement. Think about the accompanying variables to guarantee the manageability of your Airbnb business:

Monetary solidness: Consistently survey your monetary well-being and benefit. Keep a strong income, monitor expenses, and make a spending plan for showcasing, upkeep, and functional expenses.

Functional effectiveness: Streamline your cycles and frameworks to limit failures and amplify efficiency. Execute innovation answers for booking the board, correspondence, and bookkeeping.

Building solid connections: Manufacture solid associations with dependable providers, specialist organizations, and project workers. Lay out long-haul connections that guarantee reliable quality and opportune help.

Nonstop learning and improvement: Remain refreshed on industry guidelines, charge necessities, and legitimate commitments. Put resources into your own proficient turn of events and look for open doors for learning and development.

Making an Inheritance and Leave Technique

Anticipating the future and taking into account a potential leave methodology is fundamental for building a maintainable Airbnb business. Here are a few elements to consider:

Progression arranging: In the event that you expect to give your Airbnb business to people in the future, foster a reasonable progression plan. Record standard working systems, strategic policies, and any special bits of knowledge or methodologies.

Extension valuable open doors: Investigate potential open doors for development past your ongoing property. Think about getting extra properties, venturing into new areas, or enhancing your land portfolio.

Leave choices: In the event that you choose to leave the Airbnb business, assess your choices. This might incorporate selling your property, changing to long-haul rentals, or cooperating with property board organizations.

Lawful and monetary contemplations: Look for legitimate and monetary exhortation to guarantee smooth progress. Figure out charge suggestions, legally binding commitments, and any administrative prerequisites associated with leaving the business.

By exploring difficulties and zeroing in on long-haul achievement, you'll fabricate a versatile and prosperous Airbnb business. Embrace market patterns, adjust to changes, improve, foster a supportable plan of action, and plan for the future to accomplish your objectives and make an enduring effect in the business.

11

Conclusion

Congratulations! You have reached the end of "Airbnb Business Blueprint: The Ultimate Guide to Starting and Succeeding in the Airbnb Business." All through this book, we have taken you on an exhaustive excursion, furnishing you with the information, procedures, and experiences expected to lay out and flourish in the realm of Airbnb.

Beginning an Airbnb business is a thrilling undertaking, however, it accompanies its own arrangement of difficulties. By understanding the Airbnb plan of action, laying out clear objectives, and making a strong strategy, you have established areas of strength for a point for progress. You have found out about legitimate and administrative prerequisites, supporting choices, and the significance of building an expert group.

Finding the ideal property is vital, and you presently know how to recognize ideal areas, assess property postings, and arrange rent arrangements. You have acquired bits of knowledge into advancing your posting, from making convincing depictions to catching excellent photographs. Furthermore, you have figured out how to convey remarkable visitor encounters, oversee activities productively, and market your Airbnb business actually.

In the last part, we investigated the speciality of exploring difficulties and making long-haul progress. You found systems for adjusting to advertise patterns and contests, taking care of irregularity and market changes, and remaining ahead through advancement. Building a feasible plan of action and making a heritage and leave technique were likewise examined, giving you a far-reaching guide for future development and change.

Keep in mind, the outcome in the Airbnb business isn't just estimated by monetary benefits yet in addition by the positive encounters and recollections you make for your visitors. By offering remarkable friendliness, constantly working on your property and visitor benefits, and remaining sensitive to industry patterns, you will situate yourself for long-haul achievement.

As you set out on your Airbnb venture, consistently recollect the significance of adjusting to change, embracing development, and looking for potential open doors for development. The business is dynamic, and remaining current with market patterns and visitor inclinations will be basic to keep an upper hand.

Last, constructing an Airbnb business is a satisfying undertaking, however, it requires devotion, constancy, and a promise of greatness. Continue picking up, investigating additional opportunities, and refining your methodologies. Your excursion as an Airbnb is recently starting, and the opportunities for development and achievement are unending.

We want you to enjoy all that life has to offer as you leave on your enterprising experience in the realm of Airbnb. May this book act as your confided buddy and guide, engaging you to fabricate a flourishing and remunerating Airbnb business.

Blissful facilitating!

www.ingramcontent.com/pod-product-compliance
Lightning Source LLC
Chambersburg PA
CBHW072238230526
45466CB00025B/2108